Diddy Do It?
US v Sean Combs
Part I

by Matthew Russell Lee

Inner City Press

September, 2024

TABLE OF CONTENTS

Chapter 1: *Ventura v. Combs* Is Filed, Quickly Settled in SDNY

Chapter 2: Waters Part on Foley Square

Chapter 3: Bail Fight Before Magistrate Judge

Chapter 4: *Richard v. Combs, et al.*, 24-cr-6848 (KPF)

Chapter 5: Lil Rod Jones - and Epstein Echo

Chapter 6: R.Kelly (EDNY) and Donnell Russell Interlude

Chapter 7: Back to September 17, 2024

Chapter 8: Coverage

Chapter 9: Interlude: How They Got That Video?

Chapter 10: Bail Appeal Before Judge Carter

Chapter 11: Consider US v. Hadden - The Columbia ob-gyn

Chapter 12: Judge Carter Drops the Hammer

I. Ventura v. Combs Is Filed & Quickly Settled in SDNY

On November 16, 2023 a lawsuit against Sean Combs went live in the U.S. District Court for the Southern District of New York. Within days it was settled.

But the 35-page complaint remained in the PACER system. Its first page said, in red, "Trigger Warning: This document contains highly graphic information of a sexual nature, including sexual assault." Inner City Press covered it, and other cases filed in 2024: Lil Rod Jones, Adria English, Jane Doe, Crystal McKinney.

On September 17, 2024 Sean Combs was brought by US Marshals before SDNY Magistrate Judge Robyn F. Tarnofsky. He had been arrested the night before in a hotel on 57th Street and now he, through his lawyer

Marc Agnifilo, was asking to be released on $50 million bond.

Just prior to the bail fight, US Attorney Damian Williams held a press conference in 26 Federal Plaza. Inner City Press went, and asked Williams if his office would be seeking pre-trial detention on Combs (yes) and how the case compared to the prosecution of R. Kelly, which Inner City Press had also cover. This question, Williams did not answer. But we will try to, later in this text.

The bail fight before Judge Tarnofsky was detailed. Inner City Press live tweeted it - the thread is below, with background inserted about the cases and incidents the lawyers alluded to, from comparisons to the Jeffrey Epstein and Larry Ray cases, to the arson of Kid Cudi's car and bust-ups of hotel rooms in New York and Los Angeles. In many places, the prosecutors' allegations track the civil cases against Combs that Inner City Press has been covering - that is noted as well. An intro:

II. Waters Part on Foley Square

Royalty in an SUV
Part the waters of Foley Square
This brother should understand
And not crucify one of his own

Sage counsel proffers
Sage Intelligence guards
3 at 3 West Star Island
Camera filming everything

Epstein too
Tried to offer a big bond
His freak-offs in lawyers' meeting room
Then the cold corpse
Out to Gold Street - Black ain't
Going out like that

This is Part I of US v. Sean Combs.

III. Bail Fight Before Magistrate Judge

OK- now US v. Sean Combs bail fight. Inner City Press asked US Attorney Damian Williams if seeks to detain; he: Yes.

Sean Combs is now sitting at the defense table in a black shirt, with two US Marshals standing behind him. His lawyer is Marc Agnifilo.

[Inner City Press previously questioned Agnifilo when he represented leaker / whistleblower Natalie Mayflower Sours Edwards, who withheld and sealed two letters she had set to the SDNY Judge]

The prosecutors' table is full...

All rise! Magistrate Judge Robyn F. Tarnofsky presiding!

Assistant US Attorney Emily Johnson introduces other AUSAs.

Agnifilo: We represent Sean Love Combs, here beside me.

Judge Tarnofsky: Mr. Combs, you have been charged with certain crimes in an indictment. You have a right be represented by a lawyer for this proceeding and any questioning by authorities. The indictment has three counts: racketeering conspiracy including sex trafficking, forced labor, bribery, arson and obstruction of justice...

Judge: Victim-1 was forced to engage in sex acts... You are charged with knowingly transporting an individual to engage in prostitution. Counsel, have you received a copy?

Agnifilo: Yes.

Judge: Mr. Combs, how do you plead?
Combs: Not guilty.

Magistrate Judge Tarnofsky: Has Judge Carter set a conference date?

AUSA Johnson: Yes, Tuesday September 24 at 10 am.

[The first day of the UN General Assembly for what it's worth]

Judge Tarnofsky: I exclude Speedy Trial Act time until then. We will have a detention hearing

AUSA Johnson: These crimes carry a maximum sentence of life in prison or death. There is a risk of flight, and that the person will obstruct justice or attempt to intimidate a witness. This is a presumption case, based on sex trafficking.

Judge Tarnofsky: Mr. Combs, the government bears the burden of establishing that you are a danger to the community. Government?

AUSA: The defendant Sean Combs abused victims for decades. He used the vast resources of his company to commit and cover up his crimes.

AUSA: Pre-Trial Services agrees he should be detained, after interviewing him. Now he's facing significant charges, with mandatory prison time. We request an order of detention. We submitted a detailed letter this morning

AUSA: He set up freak-offs, forcing sex and masturbating during it. He also filmed some of them. He stocked the room with narcotics so that female victims would continue, for multiple days…

AUSA: The defendant committed other physical assaults, kidnapping and arson. He surrounded himself with and use firearms, including the three defaced AR-15s we seized, one in LA, two in Miami in his bedroom closet

AUSA: The indictment charges bribery and obstruction of justice. Let me give an example: March 5, 2016 at the Intercontinental Hotel in LA, disclosed in May of this year. This incident is critical: it is a recorded example of his use of force

AUSA: The victim sought to leave a freak-off and he assaulted her. When hotel security was helping the victim leave the hotel, the defendant attempted to bribe the officer with a handful of cash. The guard refused to be bought. The defendant tried to get the video

AUSA: The video disappeared from the hotel's server. It's not a coincidence. The cover up continued for another seven years. There was a civil suit in mid November 2023 that detailed this assault at the Intercontinental. The defendant denied it, called it lies…

AUSA: We fast-forward to the video being publicized - then the defendant admitted he was involved in this assault. It is clear you cannot believe him when he denies things.

[Note: This is the Cassie Ventura video; the next day on appeal to Judge Carter, AUSA Johnson will read from communications between Combs and Venture after the hallway beating.

The lawsuit is, or was, Ventura v. Combs, et al., 23-cr-10098 (DLC - Judge Denise L. Cote). It remains available on PACER, and presumably on CourtListener.

The complaint says, as to arson, that "Mr. Combs… blew up a man's car after he learned that he was romantically interested in Ms. Ventura… ran out of his apartment with a firearm in pursuit of a rival industry executive whom he learned was nearby."]

AUSA Johnson: Make no mistake: March 5 is just one example. There are numerous assaults: chocking...

AUSA: This freak-off activity is core to this case. The risk of danger in this case is acute. There has been spontaneous violence - so it is difficult to craft any conditions for release. It's this longstanding pattern of abuse, entirely undeterred

AUSA: Witnesses we have interviewed have universally expressed fear. The defendant has contacted witnesses who received grand jury subpoenas; he contacted at least one victim. This constant contact with witnesses - on Sept 10, a week ago, Dawn Richard sued...

IV. Richard v. Combs, et al., 24-cr-6848 (KPF)

[Note: That lawsuit is Richard v. Combs, et al., 24-cr-6848 (KPF - Judge Katherine Polk Failla.

The lawsuit offers corroboration, stating at 2 that "Ms. Richard witnessed Mr. Combs brutally beat his girlfriend Ms. Casandra "Cassie" Ventura... Mr. Combs threatened Ms. Richards' life with statements such as "you want to die today?" and "I end people."]

AUSA: Before a Sept 14 statement by Ms. Harper, the defendant called her 54 times in one day. Some of the way in which the defendant contacts witness and victims are meant to evade - he uses intermediaries

AUSA: The defendant cannot overcome the presumption. On obstruction, courts have revoked bail in this Circuit: Lafontaine, feeding a false narrative.

[Note: Also in SDNY, Sam Bankman-Fried of FTX, who was initially released on bail with the prosecutors' agreement, had his bail revoked when he was found to have, among other things, shared the private writings of cooperating witness and his former girlfriend

Caroline Ellison, with a reporter. It was construed as witness intimidation / obstruction of justice and Bankman-Fried was remanded to the MDC jail, where after conviction at trial and pending appellate argument he remains - with Combs and others, including Honduras' former president Juan Orlando Hernandez]

AUSA Johnson: Jeffrey Epstein was detained, on conduct going much further back in time..

V. Lil Rod Jones - and Epstein Echo

[Note: Lil Rod Jones' lawsuit in SDNY, at 33, says he "discovered that Mr. Combs has hidden cameras in every room of his house… Mr. Comb's has recordings of Defendants Lucian Charles Grainge and other celebrities, music label executives, politicians and athletes [and] every person that has attended his freak off parties….

There is more, much more, to be said about Epstein and the echoes - see below, and future parts of this work]

VI. R.Kelly (EDNY) and Donnell Russell (SDNY) Interlude

AUSA: R. Kelly was detained....

[Inner City Press covered that case too, in the Eastern District of New York - where the judge did not allow the press into the courtroom:

Inner City Press R.Kelly trial report: snoring in the (overflow) courtroom as two cousins in Homeland Security testified about R.Kelly's iPad seized incident to arrest in Trump building in Chicago; also semen DNA Cannick said could have been taken "over fence" ...

Press and public can't see jurors' reactions; on exhibits AUSA said some were "for jury only." Even other exhibits were not shown on screen.

There was also the SDNY trial of R. Kelly associate Donnell Russell, for making threats leading to the cancellation of a Manhattan screening of "Surviving R. Kelly" - when will an equivalent on Combs be released? From Inner City Press' Donnell Russell thread, July 20, 2022

OK - Trial of R.Kelly "associate" Donnell Russell set to kick off with oral arguments, after 2-day jury selection. Yesterday Judge Gardephe kept out of evidence a text about "call me Daddy." Inner City Press is covering the case(s) & will live tweet, thread below

All rise!
Judge Gardephe: I understand the lawyers have an issue?
Assistant US Attorney: Yes, we have agreed on redactions.
Judge Gardephe: Do I understand we will hear testimony today from the person who received the call?
AUSA: Yes.

Opening arguments.
Assistant US Attorney: The defendant called and said someone had a gun and would shoot up the theater. He wanted to shut down the show. You see, that show was a documentary about the defendant's boss, recording artist R.Kelly

AUSA: In that show, women said things that would expose R.Kelly and cost him money. There was a live panel discussion scheduled, to hear the women speak about R.Kelly. The defendant wanted to keep these woman quiet. This threat worked. The theater was evacuated

AUSA: That was because the defendant picked up the phone and made that threat. He knew that his words would sabotage the event. And that's exactly when happened. The defendant committed Federal crimes. That is why you're here today. That is what this trial is about.

AUSA Lara Pomerantz: "The defendant worked for R.Kelly as his manager." If R. Kelly was making lots of money, the defendant stood to gain. If not, it hurt the defendant's bottom line. Lifetime TV had produced a docu-series about R.Kelly, devastating to his career

AUSA: Lifetime partnered with a theater in NYC, to host the premiere on Dec 4, 2018. The defendant sent an email pretending to be someone else, that he invented. Why?

Because he wanted to convince Lifetime by smearing the women in the docu-series.

AUSA: On Dec 4, the defendant called the theater nine times, trying to get someone who worked at the theater on the phone. He spoke with an employee and pretended to be someone else, just like in the email. He pretended to be a lawyer representing R.Kelly

AUSA: Then the theater got an online submission from this so-called lawyer, who was the defendant, a cease and desist demand. But the event was going forward. He had a co-conspirator on the inside, named Kash Jones

AUSA: The defendant called two NYPD stations; he blocked his phone number. He called the FDNY and an affiliate. Then he called, from his home in Chicago, the theater here in Manhattan. The same employee answered. This time, the defendant said someone had a gun

AUSA: The defendant said, Someone in the event has a gun and is going to shoot up the place. The theater employee was scared. He had just been told someone was going to shoot up a theater full of people. He spoke to his managers and called 911.

AUSA: The theater was evacuated. The airing of the docu-series was cut short. There was no panel discussion. The defendant texted Kash Jones, his person on the inside, that the police may be coming. Then he texted her again & said, Delete my text about the police

AUSA: This was a terrifying inter-state threat, to sabotage an event to protect R.Kelly and his own business. As a result, he is charged in two counts: inter-state threat, and conspiracy to do the same thing

AUSA: How will we prove this to you? You'll hear from people who were at the theater that night, including the employee who took the defendant's calls.... You'll see the emails between the defendant and Kash Jones.

AUSA: You will see interviews the defendant did saying, Yes there was a threat, and that he was happy about it. This will be a short trial...

Donnell Russell's lawyer Freedman: Some of what you will hear will not be about Don Russell, but instead about R.Kelly. But this trial is not about R. Kelly - it is about Don Russell. Your job is to hear evidence. It is hard.

Freedman: You're going to have to separate out the evidence about R.Kelly. You told us, when you filled out the questionnaire, that you can put aside the information about R. Kelly and be fair and impartial.

Freedman: It's like the game of telephone - I know some of you remember it. A message gets garbled as it moves around. But some of the evidence does relate to Mr. Russell. He's an entertainment executive. In 2018 he tried to help Robert Sylvester Kelly, R. Kelly

Freedman: Mr. Russell did try to get Lifetime to cease and desist, by saying the documentary infringed on Mr. Kelly's copyright. He did contact Kash Jones. You'll see their text messages. Yes he kept calling the theater, to talk about copyright infringement

Freedman: Mr. Russell was in Chicago, so he couldn't just call NYC 911. So he called the stations. And he told Kash Jones about it. You see, it was a busy day, the theater was getting a lot of phone calls. The desk staffer got a call from a different guy...

Freedman: This other guy told the employee there was someone in the theater with a gun. The evidence is not going to be black and white. You're not going to hear that call, only the employee about it. Remember, the game of telephone.

Freedman: You'll hear the 911 call, but not the threat call. At some point, the police did come. And someone said, let's look at the phone log. The employee didn't know which call had been the threat. But Mr. Russell's name was on the call log.

Freedman: We are asking you to pay close attention to the evidence. There is evidence he was pleased with the result, which he had hoped for. But it doesn't show that he made that threat. In that interview, he'd going to say he was raising copyright.

Freedman: A lot of the evidence, I'm not going to dispute. It may not make you think highly of him. You may not think it was a good idea. But you're going to have to decide if there's enough evidence about the threat call to find that he made it.

Freedman: Mr. Russell is not guilty. Thank you.
Judge Gardephe: First witness.
AUSA Davis: The government calls Isaiah Hemingway... What do you do for work?
Hemingway: I worked at the theater, it was a members-only club on 25th Street between Madison and Park Ave

AUSA: Did you attend an event involving R.Kelly?

Hemingway: Yes, the premiere of Surviving R. Kelly.

AUSA: Did you recognize anyone?

Hemingway: R. Kelly's ex-wife.

AUSA: Then what happened?

Hemingway: They suddenly said we had to evacuate. I was scared.

AUSA: Show the witness and counsel Gov Exhibit 202. What is it?

Hemingway: A picture I took of the screening room.

AUSA: The government offers Exhibit 202.

Judge Gardephe: Any objection?

Freedman: No.

Judge Gardephe: It is admitted [into evidence]

AUSA: No further questions.

Judge Gardephe: Cross examination.

Freedman: We've never met, correct?

Hemingway: Correct.

Freedman: When you met with the US on

June 23, you weren't sure if anyone said there had been a threat, right?

Hemingway: I don't know the date

Freedman: You read the press, about a gun threat, right?

Hemingway: Yes, I read the press. But I knew if we had to evacuate, I knew there had to have been a threat. I saw law enforcement.

Freedman: Even the evacuation, it took you a couple of minutes to decide it was serious, right?

Hemingway: I was just thinking in the spur of the moment.

Freedman: You yourself never heard a threat, right?

Hemingway: No. But I knew it was serious.

Freeman: Nothing further.

Judge Gardephe: Next witness.

AUSA Pomerantz: First some photographs, we'll put them on a board: Donnell Russell, Kash Jones...

Judge Gardephe: If no objection, go right ahead.

AUSA: And the 911 call, as evidence.
Freedman: No objection.

AUSA Davis, to next witness: Where do you work?
Witness: The US Attorney's Office, SDNY.
AUSA Davis: Did you work on the investigation of Donnell Russell?
Witness: Yes. I downloaded YouTube videos.

Now AUSA is playing an interview given by Donnell Russell. [Inner City Press has requested copies of all exhibits in this case, and the Josh Schulte and Larry Ray / Isabella Pollok cases, from the SDNY - still waiting]
Judge Gardephe: We'll take a break.

They've back.
AUSA: What is this?
Witness: A communication from Don Russell to June Barrett.
AUSA: Pull up Gov't Exhibit 1408. Who's this from?
Witness: From June Barrett to Don Russell.

AUSA: And the attachment, 1408A.
Witness: It's an invoice.

AUSA: What's this?
Witness: Messages between Kash Jones and Donnell Russell on December 4.
AUSA: This could be a natural stopping point...
Judge Gardephe: Let's go to 1 pm.
AUSA: Of course your Honor. OK, what is this call?
Witness: It's to the theater.

Programming note: Judge Gardephe has called the lunch break in US v. Donnell Russell; Inner City Press is renewing its effort to get and publish the exhibits being rushed through by AUSA Davis, watch this feed.

OK, jury is back from break.
AUSA Davis: I want to focus on communications between 7:12 and 7:27 pm. What's this?
Witness: Donnell Russell made a phone call. And uses star 67.
AUSA Davis: Pull up Gov't Exhibit 902.

What's this?

Witness: Russell using another number.

AUSA: At this time, we would like to play Govt Exhibit 701.

Judge Gardephe: Go ahead.

911 call is played, from Adrian, citing "an anonymous phone call... I hope you understand my urgency."

Now prosecution plays video of Donnell Russell saying he sent cease and desist communications to Lifetime TV and others.

AUSA Davis: No further questions.

Judge Gardephe: Cross examination.

Freedman: Where do you live - the Bronx or Manhattan?

AUSA: Objection.

Freedman: Do you live in NYC?

Witness: I no longer live in NYC.

Judge Gardephe: You need to speak up Mr. Freedman.

Freedman: I'm a bit trapped in here [in plexiglass COVID protection booth] You

worked with the prosecutors on all this, right?
Witness: Yes.

Next witness is former Neuehouse Member Services Manager Adrian Krasniqi, until 2021.
AUSA: What was your job in 2018?
Krasniqi: Member Services Manager.
AUSA: What did you do at the front desk?
Krasniqi: Answer emails and the phone.

AUSA: On Dec 4, 2018 what was there?
Krasniqi: A screening of Surviving R. Kelly in our screening room. There were about 70 people.
AUSA: The call you received, what did the caller sound like?
Krasniqi: Deep voice, professional. The call was brief.

AUSA: What Gov Exhibit 1203?
Krasniqi: A Post-It note with my handwriting on it. It says a representative of R.Kelly's legal team, cease and desist, copyright, 6:32 pm.
AUSA: What did you do?

Krasniqi: Spoke to my manager. She said, tell 'em to put it in writing.

AUSA: What was the next call?
Krasniqi: A threat about a gun. The voice was deep and serious, very much like a thug.
AUSA: Did you think it was the same person as the copyright threat?
Krasniqi: They were similar deep male voices.

AUSA: What did you do?
Krasniqi: Contacted a colleague Kastriot Pacarada. We flagged down our general manager Alison Hunt. She told me to call the police. I called 911.
[911 call is played]

911 operator: So there were shots fired in the building?
Krasniqi: No, there was an anonymous call about a gun.
AUSA: In 2018 did you sometimes use drugs?
Krasniqi: I smoked weed. But not that day.

AUSA: No further questions.
Judge Gardephe: Cross examination.
Freedman: You spoke a lot with the prosecutors - seven times since June, right?
Krasniqi: I guess.
Freedman: And that night, you called your dad?
Krasniqi: I don't remember.

Freedman: And the first caller, about cease and desist, the caller sounded professional, you said, right?
Krasniqi: He sounded like a lawyer.
Freedman: And the second caller, you called him a thug?
Krasniqi: He had a Brooklyn accent. I was living in Brooklyn.

Freedman: Is this a photo of the phone at the front desk?
AUSA: Objection!
Judge Gardephe: Overruled.
Krasniqi: It looks like it.

Freedman asks about mushrooms and acid. On re-direct, AUSA Pomerantz ask if he took

either that day (no) & if when sober he has a good memory (he says he does).
And with that, the trial day is over.

VII. Back to September 17, 2024

AUSA Johnson: Keith Raniere, detained on all three grounds, even though the violence was committed by others. His incentive to flee changed when he was arrested last night

AUSA: The defendant is a wealthy man, it allows him to flee quickly and without detection. His counsel have taken steps to minimize flight risk, to set him up for the argument made today. But then his incentives were entirely different. He flew to New York 2 weeks ago

AUSA: He had what appear to be narcotics, found in his hotel last night. Pink powder, that have previously tested positive for Ecstasy and other drugs.

[Note: Lil Rod Jones' lawsuit, at 30, defines "Tuci" as "a pink drug that is a combination of ecstasy and cocaine."]

This is a heartland detention case. His package is woefully inadequate, it only focuses on flight risk

AUSA: The Government has spoken to over 50 witnesses; we have sworn out warrants for cloud accounts. The searches have yielded 90 cell phones and 30 other devices including a surveillance system. The freak-offs are corroborated. 300 Grand Jury subpoenas...

AUSA: The defendant poses a danger to these proceedings, through obstruction. He should be detained pending trial.
Judge: Mr. Agnifilo?
Agnifilo: I'm going to address the Government's letter. But first - on September 5, Mr. Combs flew to New York

Agnifilo: We could tell an indictment was coming in the Fall, from our meetings with the prosecutors' chiefs. My client flew to New

York. I told the prosecutors, I'd like him to have the opportunity to turn himself in

Agnifilo: We got involved in this case in March 2024. We've been doing our own investigation. On March 13 I reached out to my colleagues at US Attorney's Office and asked to meet. The November 2023 lawsuit, seems connected - it got attention, they read the papers

Agnifilo: After the raids, we took Mr. Combs passport, on April 1. After that, any time he traveled domestically, we told the prosecutors. A trip to graduations in California. Another one for white water rafting. We wanted to build trust, to surrender

Agnifilo: The March 25 raids were frightening - lasers pointed at his children, they were marched out of the front of the house, with news reporters and helicopters. Handcuffed for two hours, completely innocent. We did not want that to happen again

Agnifilo: Mr. Combs flew to New York to say, You want me, I know you want me. Here he is. We were worried that he had an airplane. We said, we have to sell it. There is a financial management company that deals with these issues. We're trying

Agnifilo: Why are we trying to sell the plane? It's not our first rodeo. The plane, someone else is using it, from LA to Teterboro, tonight. Just my luck. I wouldn't have the temerity to come here and ask for freedom if I didn't have the passports

AUSA: There's one victim in Count 2, the sex trafficking charge. Mr. Combs wrote a very large check to someone he was in a relationship with for ten years. People got in line for their checks. I had no idea: 12 victims? I didn't know. I'm happy there's only one

Agnifilo: This case, we think, is eminently manageable. Pre-Trial Services says he has a criminal record. But he was acquitted. He is ready to do that again. What is Mr. Combs doing in NY? He's here for treatment and therapy

Agnifilo: Mr. Combs is not a perfect person. These toxic relationships were mutual. Now he is trying to be better for the rest of his days. If there's one thing we've seen, we should stand with people who are trying to get the help they need

AUSA: Somehow this hotel footage found its way out. I wonder how that happened. We didn't have it. The government had it. It got out, on a day Donald Trump didn't have any court proceedings. Mr. Combs saw it and issued an apology. He wanted to do it

Agnifilo: Two people were in a hotel room. An issue that Mr. Combs had more than one girlfriend, okay? Victim-1 was looking through his phone and saw that - then hit him in the head with a cellphone, and took his clothing. So he comes out in a towel

Agnifilo: These two people were in love. Victim-1 ended up marrying the trainer that

Mr. Combs got for her. They had been cheating on each other for years. But now she had two kids with the trainer. Years later, she realized she had a good thing with Mr. Combs

Agnifilo: She has her lawyer call his lawyer and say, She has written a book. But if you want to buy the rights, you'll have the rights, for $30 million. We have a recorded conversation. It did not go well for her and the lawyer. November 2023, she sues

Agnifilo: When he contacts witnesses, it's not to stop a criminal investigation, it's to not be seen that way. Why is it depicted as a one-sided thing? There are 30 million reasons, a dollar a piece. She said, I'm going to write a book, you can buy the rights.

Agnifilo: This Dawn Richard lawsuit, and Ms. Harper, from the same band. The lawsuit says, He did a couple of inappropriate things. Ms. Harper said, That was not my experience. That is not intimidation. It's divergent recollections. There's nothing wrong with that

Agnifilo: I'm not even sure Dawn Richard is a witness in this case. My client hasn't done a darn thing.... We have interviewed at least six of these males, we asked did it seem non-consensual, anyone too drunk or too high, they all said No

Agnifilo: Is it sex trafficking if everyone wants to be there? No. We don't want the Federal government in our bedroom. The kidnapping? We spoke to the victim, she didn't use that word to us. One day it may be heard. Mr. Combs employs a security company.

Agnifilo: Mr. Combs has nothing to do with how guns are kept in his house. He needs security, in the sections of LA and Miami he lives in. Did they do it wrong? Not for us to say. Not his gun. R. Kelly? That involved children. They cannot consent.

Agnifilo: Jeffrey Epstein? Children.

[Note - arrested after the death of Epstein in the MCC, Ghislaine Maxwell did not get bail, and is now serving her sentence in a Federal prison in Florida, her appeal denied by the Second Circuit Court of Appeals in September 2024.

Lil Rod Jones' lawsuit asserts, at 29, that Defendant Kristina Khorram is the Ghislaine Maxwell to Sean Combs' Jeffrey Epstein. What say the SDNY prosecutors, who arrested Maxwell after Epstein was carried out of the MCC?]

Agnifilo: Keith Raniere? Children. We have a substantial bail package. Some family members are here. They love him. A $50 million bond, secured by a $48 million piece of property. On August 20, we paid off the $18 million mortgage

Agnifilo: One day we're have a fair trial. We have substantial defenses to each of these charges. Mr. Combs is handling this head on. He's become a punching bag. He's built businesses from scratch. His father was killed when he was 2 years old. He earned all of it

Agnifilo: Mr. Combs has earned this court's trust. I have nothing else to say.

Judge: Ms. Johnson, any rebuttal?

AUSA Johnson: Defense counsel has his critique of law enforcement. But he has not rebutted the presumption that the defendant should be detained

AUSA: Three days after the November 2023 lawsuit, the defendant is recorded saying he doesn't want to talk on the phone, it might be tapped. He uses armed security - with defaced AR-15s stored in the defendant's personal closet? Absurd.

AUSA: For the record, we are proceeding on a theory of lack of consent, that she was coerced to participate in those sex acts.
Judge: He wouldn't be a danger, would he, if he only engaged in these behaviors with

consenting adults?

AUSA: We have the hallway video

Agnifilo: This is a slippery slope. The Government is going to say she was coerced - she had to say that to go for the $30 million. We have a serious bail package. I hope your Honor can see that Mr. Combs has done things to show that he is trustworthy.

Agnifilo: I am asking you to trust me. I have my eye on him. We speak 5 times a day. I want to thank Your Honor.

Judge Tarnofsky: Thank you. I am going to take a short recess and invite Pre-Trial Services to join me in the robing room. [Judge leaves the courtroom

[With Judge out of courtroom with Pre-Trial Services rep, Combs is sitting at defense table with Agnifilo, who is gesturing in front of him. ...

Note: Earlier in the week, Judge Tarnofsky after a similar time in the robing room released a Bronx superintendent alleged to have sold guns and drugs from his basement office. So - would it be the same for Combs?

Judge is back.]

Judge: In this case - oh sorry, counsel's not here. My apologies.

[Prosecutors file back in, to the front table]
Judge: Mr. Agnifilo, do we need to wait for your partner?
Agnifilo: I really appreciate it.

Then:

Judge Tarnofsky : In this case I find the presumption has not been rebutted

[So, Sean Combs will be detained]

Judge: There was been significant violence, and weapons around. Also coercion of witnesses even gentle coercion can be effective. The type of behavior we're talking about happens behind closed doors. I think your family members for coming, but I cannot release him

AUSA: For the record, Mr. Combs was arrested at 8:25 pm last night. Judge: Thank you. We are adjourned.

VIII. Coverage

After that decision, and that thread, Inner City Press got calls from all over. Some of the pick-up coverage was accurate, some was not.

Sept 18, 2024, Variety, "Sean 'Diddy' Combs Denied Bail in Appeal Hearing, Will Remain in Custody," by Steven J. Horowitz, "During the bail appeal hearing, documented by Inner City Press'

Matthew Russell Lee, prosecutors reiterated points from the indictment that he drugged victims"

Sept 18, 2024, Rolling Stone, "Sean Combs' Alleged Witness Tampering," by Cheyenne Roundtree, "the woman allegedly texted Combs that reading Ventura's lawsuit felt like she was "reading my own sexual trauma," reported Inner City Press' Matthew Russell Lee"

Sept 18, 2024, Complex, "Diddy Arrest: Bags of Pink Powder Drug Allegedly Found in Hotel Room," by Trace William Cowen, "Inner City Press' Matthew Russell Lee, meanwhile, was also on hand for Tuesday's hearing, reporting that Assistant U.S. Attorney Emily Johnson argued that Diddy was a flight risk"

Sept 18, 2024, Hot 97, "Diddy Reportedly Accuses Cassie Of Cheating Before Abuse," "According to Diddy's attorney, Marc Agnifilo, said she had been sleeping with her trainer for years, according to Inner City Press"

Sept 17, 2024, VIBE, "Diddy's Attorney Claims Cassie Hit Him With Cellphone Ahead Of Hotel Hallway Attack," by Jessica Bennett, "Reporter Matthew Russell Lee of Inner City Press shared Agnifilo's statements via X/Twitter"

Sept 17, 2024, Hot New Hip Hop, "Diddy's Lawyer Alleges That Cassie Hit Diddy Prior To Hotel Hallway Attack," by Elias Andrews, "Marc Agnifilo addressed the infamous security video in which his client attacked ex-girlfriend, Cassie. He then tried to make a case against Cassie. Inner City Press shared Agnifilo's statements on Twitter"

IX. Interlude: How They Got That Video?

"I came up hard
Now I jet Miami
I like to make 'em freak-off
Yes I came up hard

She ran in the hotel
I wasn't finished yet
I kicked her again and again
How they got that video?

Easy to prosecute
When you got an army
Serial numbers filed off
Now they used against me

I paid this cat to get me out
He told me, Sell the plane
He can't even convince Tarnofsky
We'll try again with Carter"

X. Bail Appeal Before Judge Carter

OK- now US v. Sean Combs bail appeal.

[In high-ceilinged Courtroom 110, Sean Combs is at defense table, still in black shirt (not MDC tan uniform). Two US Marshals seated behind him.
Waiting on Judge Andrew L. Carter…

All rise!
Government?
AUSA Emily Johnson: The freak-offs were elaborate. They began in 2009 and extended into this year. These freak-offs were arranged with his entourage. The defendant used narcotics so that the victims would continue: ketamine, GHB and others

[Note: Lil Rod's complaint, at 7, says he as "irrefutable evidence of the acquisition, use and distribution of ecstasy, cocaine, GHB, ketamine, marijuana and mushrooms… Mr.

Combs Chief of Staff, Kristina Khorram instructing her staff to retrieve drugs so she can provide it to Mr. Combs for his consumption"]

AUSA: The defendant would record these freak-offs at least in part to use them to blackmail. We have an email, a victim says You were going to make me - I'm not going to say it on the public record - or you were going to leak some F.O. shit

AUSA: A different victim wrote, He said he was going to expose me with the sex tape, I was drugged.
That's just two example. And so it's rich when the defendant submission filed today accuses the victim of extorting. He's the only extorter

AUSA: We seized six guns, they were in the defendant's home and he had access to them. We are focused on the defaced guns in defendant's closet. This is not about security but dangerousness. The security team is the same one he says would monitor him

AUSA: The head of his security has now been served with a subpoena, given what we've learned about his role in the offense conduct. Now, about the hotel assault - yesterday defense counsel called it a fight in a relationship. But it's trafficking

AUSA: The defendant had a freak-off on March 5, 2016. We have evidence there was one commercial sex worker there in the room, during the assault. She isn't even wearing shoes. She is in danger. Defendant storms out in a towel

AUSA: We have a message from the Victim, I still have crazy bruising. He claims he wanted to get his clothes back. But that's not what happened her. She tried to escape a room with the defendant and a commercial sex worker - she fled without shoes

AUSA: Immediately after the assault, the defendant sent these messages: Call me, the cops are here. I got six kids. Yo, please call, I am surrounded. You gonna abandon me all alone.

The defendant knew he had done something that could elicit police response

AUSA: He covered up what he did. This year, after the surveillance video came out, only then did he admit that it was him. Yesterday it was claimed that his clothes were taken - but that's not what happened. Why drag the victim back down the hall to the room?

AUSA: The indisputable evidence makes clear you cannot take the defendant at his word. March 5, 2016 is far from the defendant's lone act of violence and obstruction. Freak-off activity is the core of this case. They use force, coercion and drugs

AUSA: Our investigation is ongoing. Half a dozen escorts are just the tip of the iceberg of the number of escorts who have participated in these freak-offs. This case is charged a sex trafficking by force, fraud and coercion. The acts were not consensual.

XI. Consider US v. Hadden - The Columbia ob-gyn

AUSA: Consider US v. Hadden - The Columbia ob-gyn

Remand, January 2023

OK - now after guilty verdict on four counts of sexually abusing patients, (ex) Doctor Robert Hadden faces remand hearing -

Judge Berman: I could take written submissions on the request for remand...
Assistant US Attorney: If you will remand him pending the decision. We have victims present who wish to speak.
Judge: Of course. Now?
Berman's lawyer: May I be heard?
AUSA: He abused trust

AUSA: He abused victims from the late 1980s to 2012 - even after that, Columbia let him return and practice medicine. He continued assaults. He abused a pregnant victim. He conducted an exam, pulled her toward him, and pulled her pants down [and more]

AUSA: Hadden claimed he was indigent. But in 2020, this Court found he arranged transfers of $1.25 million to his immediate family members and that it undermined his claim for court-appointed lawyers. The defendant did all he could to avoid punishment

AUSA: The Court can have no confidence he won't use transferred resources to avoid prison time. The Court cannot trust him. In pre-trial filings, he argued his state plan was not voluntary. Then he changed tack. He wrote that his victims lied. He can't be trusted

AUSA: We are prepared to call victims.
Judge Berman: I'll hear from the defense briefing, then victims.
Hadden's lawyer: These are considerations for sentencing. The only question is risk of flight. There is none. He has shown up here [points at him in front row]

Hadden's lawyer: He has not left the US since 1984. He came every day and stuck it out. He won't travel due to is wife with diabetes, and his grown son who is mentally disabled. Mr. Hadden bathes him. He will not leave them in the lurch

Hadden's lawyer: He's living on disability, going to church & the grocery store. His co-signer is here-
Judge Berman: Is that a relative?
Hadden's lawyer: No.
[Note: so, even sex criminal's co-signer is not confidential. So how is Bankman-Fried requesting it?]

Hadden's lawyer: He faces a significant sentence, he is aware of that. Don't attribute to Mr. Hadden my litigation strategy.
Judge Berman: This is complicated. I don't want to shoot from the hip. I will want a written submission on bail / remand.

Hadden's lawyer: His mental medication is not available in the MDC. He would remain out--

Judge Berman: I am going to do that. But be aware, there is a sense that Mr. Hadden has always presented reasons he can't afford a lawyer, can't go to jail

Judge Berman: He needs a Plan B. If people need to be assisted, he'll have to put that in place a.s.a.p. As soon as his name comes up, people are mystified he pled in state court and got a conditional discharge, unheard of. Come up with a Plan B.

Hadden's lawyer: The statute only says risk of flight, not "did you get too lucky last time."
Judge: I do remember that assets were transferred, multi-million dollars.
Hadden's lawyer: His inheritance. He disclaimed it to his children. He didn't move it overseas

Judge Berman: He needs Plan B and he needs it right away. Do the victims wish to speak?
AUSA: Give us a moment.
[The stated decision that Hadden will walk out of court today has changed the mood.]

AUSA: Some defendants cut their [GPS] bracelets...

Judge Berman: What about danger to community?

Hadden's lawyer: The government has not argued it.

AUSA: The first victim...

Victim-1: I have been doing this since June 2012. I want to thank you for what you just said. Hadden has continued to live a life at home

Victim-1: We walk the earth tortured by what this person did. Thank you for listening to us.

AUSA: Next victim is Marissa Hoechstetter.

Ms. Hoechstetter: I went to see Mr. Hadden because I was a friend of his niece - he talked about her as he abused me.

Ms. Hoechstetter: I worked to pass a law to allow changing of names on birth certificate, to take his name off. He delivered my children by C-section. He was the first to touch them. I had to see that, when they registered for school. Other victims are watching.

Judge Berman: The civil proceeding, what is the time frame?

Ms. Hoechstetter: I helped pass the law that allows the one-year look-back. It is an evolving situation. His evasion of accountability continues to be painful for many many people and their families.

AUSA: Next is Jessica Sell Chambers.

Jessica Sell Chambers: What he did to me has impacted me for 20 years, his giddiness as he touched me. That is PTSD. 210 women with 15 years of memories. He has impacted thousands of years. Each time he has been given a pass

Jessica Sell Chambers: The ante has just been upped. He has more motivation to do any number of things. He has sentenced us to thousands of years. He should be taken into custody to avoid him harming himself. This is what is owed to us.

AUSA: Next...

Robyn Bass Lavender: I went to Barnard College. Understanding now what he did to me... when I see doctors now... A lot of emotions and confusion... We've known for ten years, and he's just gone on living his life. We all take care of our families

Robyn Bass Lavender: He shouldn't have another 90 days to live in his house, eating his own food. It's time to go to jail.

AUSA: Next is Liz Hall.

Liz Hall (sobs) I've told my story often, but I've yet to actually be heard. I was 21. He gave me free birth control

Liz Hall: I have two children whom I also take care of. His assault of me was in his closed office. He told me how my body came back, he jumped up and assaulted me. I had already seen him for 10 years.

Liz Hall: I was so happy when he was arrested. But he was immediately released. He has never been held accountable. Every woman who has seen him was a victim -

that's 1000s. He shows no remorse. I was here every day. My job might be on the line

Liz Hall: I just don't want to be assaulted by him anymore. Please detain him.
AUSA: Next...
Laurie Maldonado: I'm new to using my name. It makes me stand taller and prouder. I want to thank the women here. They have changed laws. I have been here every day.

Maldonado: 48 hours before my child was born, he shoved a fist in me. It was sexual assault. My husband asked, Were you violated? I said Yes. But I didn't understand, I could barely walk. This is so painful. My son is so beautiful. Hadden could have harmed him

Madonado: He needs to be behind bars as soon as possible.
[Two of Hadden's lawyer are whispering to each other]
AUSA: Next is Dayna Solomon.
Dayna Solomon: He is the most insidious

human being I've ever met. I didn't believe he'd been arrested.

Dayna Solomon: I saw when he was allowed to come back to work. He shoved his finger up me. So insidious. It feels like I was raped in my sleep. It's haunting. How can he get to go home and grieve with this family and taper off his medication. We don't get to

Dayna Solomon: Why not just get rid of him now? It's like the day he came back to work, letting him go out there.
AUSA: Now, not in her true name, we'll provide the name to defense counsel.
Victim: I was to be part of the initial trial - then he got a plea deal

Victim: I haven't been able to be a mom to my kids because of what he did. I have debilitating migraines. He should have a Plan B already. I was 20, I was a virgin, I went to Hadden to regulate my period because I was engaged. I grew up in an Orthodox household

Victim: I bled after the visit, not on my wedding night. I have had three babies, three live babies. He would check if I was dilated, from the very first month. I didn't realize it until I had my fourth child with another doctor.

Victim: In July 2011 he just grabbed my breast. I looked down. He was wearing khaki Dockers and he had an erection. He had milk in his beard. I ran out of there, loudly on my phone. I told my husband I'm never having any more kids. I would have had a larger family

Victim: His excuses were really calculated. He said I was allergic to latex so he could use his fingers. His excuse is clever. He should be taken into custody now, no more free air. I haven't been able to breathe. Give us peace.

AUSA: I read the statement of Emily Anderson. She urges the court to detain the defendant. So does Gabriela Diaz, she says she has been serving a life sentence. Every day he is free is a risk, to flee or harm himself. Detain him tonight, with hearing tomorrow 9 am

Judge Berman: Why has no one raised danger to the community?
[Here's an idea: possible suicide as risk of flight]

Judge Berman: I think it's too narrow a view. The victims' story is danger to the community. What I'm suggesting is that the focus may be off.
AUSA: There is a risk he could harm another victim.
Judge Berman: You're probably more schooled that I am in the case law

Judge Berman: I haven't heard from pre-trial, now post-trial. What is the psychological regime that Mr. Hadden has followed?
Pre-Trial: He sees a psychiatrist, and a therapist.
Judge Berman: What days? I have a license but I don't practice, except here.

Judge Berman: My mind is open but what is astonishing to me, it's almost inconceivable someone with those compulsion can't turn the switch and not be a danger to the community.
Hadden's lawyer: He's registered as a sex offender. The FBI has torn his life apart

Judge Berman: It's inconceivable to me that there is not a danger, maybe to himself [Again: suicide risk as risk of flight?]
Judge Berman: I'm not concerned about Second Circuit cases right now. If I'm right and they say different, they're wrong.

Hadden's lawyer: Tomorrow morning is too fast, I have a proffer to make
[For Ms. White in US v. Billy Ortega?]
Judge Berman: Hearing Feb 1 at noon.
AUSA: We urge him detained until then.
Judge Berman: He's not going to run, he'd be the most known person if he did

AUSA: Presumably he is distraught, he urges him detained until the hearing.
Judge Berman: I believe that's not appropriate, we do not have enough

information.

AUSA: The defendant has not met his burden.

Judge: Briefs Monday at noon. Then Feb 1, everyone is invited

[Note: There are at times bail appeals to the 2d Circuit. No stay for that being requested here. Yet?]

Judge Berman: In the submissions, I also want Plan B. I think that's it for today. See you February 1.

Inner City Press' thread, July 2023

OK - Dirty Doc Hadden sentencing now continued @SDNYLIVE. Yesterday Judge Berman said he "proposes" 20 year sentence. But Federal Defender objected to victims, state lines - so it is continuing today, Inner City Press will live tweet (or x), thread below

Assistant US Attorney: Defendant has not been rehabilitated. At least 25 years are necessary and appropriate.

Federal Defender: We contest whether the conclusion it was abuse was 1 the Court should rely on. We filed something under seal, something Columbia cleared

Federal Defender: We are saying the witness' testimony was based on her own history of abuse. So we ask the Court to not consider those incidents.

Judge: My position is in yesterday's transcript. I found it credible, the testimony. The defense could have crossed

Judge Berman: I endorsed AUSA Kim's letter and said the sentencing would not be postponed. That was about yesterday. You can show the letter to the jury - I mean, the media [in the jury box - here is the endorsement on the letter.

Judge Berman: So let me say, I intend to sentence this defendant to 20 years. [Yesterday he said he "proposed" twenty years - we're getting closer to finality - although Federal Defenders seems sure to appeal the upward variance, perhaps why this has taken so long

Federal Defender: There is no reason for drug testing.
Judge Berman: I did put it in and I do put it in in many of the sentences that I do irrespective of, or acknowledging that the Probation Department may not have included it, there is some history in his family

Federal Defender: I believe this sentence violates the Sixth and Fifth Amendments.
Judge Berman: Mr. Hadden, anything? No? Government?
AUSA: What about the collection of DNA? & SORNA?
Judge Berman: OK - now I'll impose sentence: it's twenty years, 240 months

Judge Berman: This is a 177 month upward variance given the serious & the need for punishment and deterrence. Any legal reasons I can't?
Federal Defender: For the reasons I have previously-

Judge: I appreciate that.

FD: We want Otisville or Devens.

Back to September 18, 2024, US v. Combs

XII. Judge Carter Drops the Hammer

AUSA: And consider US v [Larry] Ray [see Inner City Press book, the Weasels of Wall Street]

AUSA: The defense is arguing that anyone in a freak-off wanted to be there. That's not the law. When people are threatened with exposure, and are beaten, they cannot consent. That is trafficking. Victims' heads were slammed against car windows

AUSA: Here are some texts: when you get fucked up, you knock me around. I'm not a

rag doll. I'm someone's child.
We have witnesses who witnessed the injuries. This conduct happened behind closed door, in houses, hotel rooms and cars. Judge Tarnofsky was concerned

AUSA: Judge Tarnofsky found that she did not believe defense counsel can control the defendant... Consider the Mercedes case in this Circuit, reversing a decision to release a defendant. Let's turn to obstruction. Witnesses have expressed extreme fear of him

AUSA: They have directly contacted a victim in November 2023. Constant contact with witnesses to the charged conduct, after subpoena, before government interviews. Two of these examples are, there are communications between the defendant and a witness, 13 contacts

Judge Carter: 13 contacts with two people?
AUSA Johnson: Sorry, 14 contacts between the defendant and the witness. Also, he outreached to a witness he had not been in

contact with for several years, after the grand jury subpoena. He used intermediaries

AUSA: He recorded the conversation on another person's device... In November 2023 he twice called a victim. On Nov 19, he received a text from this other person in response. It reads, I feel like I'm reading my own sexual trauma. 3 pages, my experience

AUSA: The defendant called her and gaslit her, trying to convince her it has been consensual. He repeatedly said he was not supposed to be speaking on the phone, he tells the witness not to text him. The defendant said if support, nothing to worry about: money

AUSA: The defendant wrote, his financial adviser should not make a mistake and not get that rent paid - this was obstruction. We cite US v. Lafontaine, a defendant who fed a false narrative. That's what's going on here.

AUSA: I'll go over the cases -
Judge Carter: That's not necessary. I'm

familiar with those cases.

AUSA: A recent civil suit. Last week Dawn Richard filed a civil suit. She was in a band, also with Ms. Harper. Ms. Harper issued a statement- after 128 phone contacts

AUSA: We didn't deal with Lawrence Ray's case - Magistrate Judge Fox ordered detention, even on one victim. But the judge found that corroborated by documentary evidence.

Judge: Anything else?

AUSA: A few more things.

Judge: How many?

AUSA: 3 minutes

AUSA: Traveling to New York does not address danger to the community. I am here seeking detention. But I note that the bail package does not have enough conditions that focus on obstruction. And it couldn't - he's been involving other people.

AUSA: The defendant should be detained pending trial.

Judge: Defense?

Combs' lawyer Marc Agnifilo: Let me start with Ms. Harper. I was called by her and a lawyer. I said, Do what you want, make a statement or not. I later found out that she did.

Combs' 2d lawyer Teny Geragos: Ms. Harper felt she was being besmirched. We did speak with her, at 2 am on the 11th.
Judge: After speaking, what would be the reason for Mr. Combs to continue contacting her?
Geragos: She was concerned she was in the media

Agnifilo: I have brought today the head of Sage Intelligence. We are proposing that Sage Intelligence personnel, all former law enforcement, will be monitoring the residence of Mr. Combs, 24/7. They will have one or two employees there at all times

Agnifilo: There will be a visitor log, only pre-approved could come in. We could give the list to the court. Mr. Combs will not have a cell phone or access to the internet. That way, no witness intimidation, completely nullified.

Agnifilo: Having Sage Intelligence on site, we'll do what we have to do, even three there. If don't believe that Mr. Combs' actions in coming to New York are only about risk of flight. It shows he is deeply respectful of the court's authority. He is responsible

Agnifilo: Mr. Combs knew he was under investigation, and gave us his passport. This is not defense lawyer theater. We took the passports of five of his family members. We have a letter of intent to sell his airplane. We had 3 buyers who didn't work out

Judge: Can you get to the point?
Agnifilo: It shows he's trustworthy. He's not a defendant who says, Come find me. In Maxwell and Epstein -
Judge: How does that relate to danger and obstruction? If he was aware in April, why was he contacting witnesses?

Agnifilo: A woman contacted him, said she'd gotten a subpoena. We told him, don't speak to her.
Judge: Talk to me about danger.
Agnifilo: People who are a danger are people who are contemptuous of the court. But Mr. Combs has never been contemptuous of the court.

Agnifilo: He had a case in New York in 1999, he came to court every time. He shows up on time.
Judge: Under your plan would he will have employees?
Agnifilo: They handle his finances. They are in California.
Judge: Would he be able to leave his residence?
A: No

Judge: And the security, they could be there in the house?
Agnifilo: Yes. In shifts. We could put cameras filming 24 hours a day. They could do spot checks he doesn't use the internet. We

can make it as secure as we need to make it. There are already cameras there

Judge: That video is troubling. He was 40 something years old

Agnifilo: He realized he has a problem with drug addiction and anger. He went into a rehab program for a period of time. The woman in the video also went into rehab at around the same time

Agnifilo: They loved each other. The written messages are heartbreaking. The sex and the violence were totally separate, motivated by separate things. They way they chose to be intimate, they would bring a third person on. They chose that

Judge: What does that have to do with him punching her, throwing a vase at her - what's love got to do with that?

Agnifilo: That was jealousy from infidelity- in both directions, Mr. Combs & this other person. The violence is from that.

Judge: What is your point?

Judge: And you say, they invited a third person in - if that person is a commercial sex worker, and they travel across state lines, isn't that a problem?

Agnifilo: I've spoken with the agency, they say they are not paid for sex, but if they feel like it.

Agnifilo: The former government of New York, he did this - and he was not prosecuted. They are prosecuting Mr. Combs for it.

Judge: Let's get back to that video and the physical beating. Why isn't that relevant to dangerousness?

Agnifilo: It's not sex trafficking

Agnifilo: Even if you don't trust him, trust the bond package - $50 million bond, no internet, Sage - that will give the court comfort that he is not a flight risk. Then he can prepare for his trial. We had known this was coming. He could have run in March

Agnifilo: He was an actual altar boy -
Judge: How far back are you going?
Agnifilo: He watches a sermon every day.

[Note: Lil Rod's complaint, at 8, cites "Mr. Combs detailing how he planned to leverage his relationship with Bishop T.D. Jakes to soften the impact on his public image of Cassie Ventura's lawsuit.]

Agnifilo: He has done a great deal to earn the court's trust. I ask you to release him.

Judge: I've heard from the parties, I find that the government have proven the defendant is a danger. Regarding the bail package, it is insufficient even on risk of flight.
[Sean Combs will remain detained.]

Judge: So let's do the initial conference.
AUSA: The discovery will include photographs of physical evidence, from the March searches and from this week, including freak-off supplies. There are a large number of electronic devices.

AUSA: We have 35 full extractions ready to produce to the defense. We'd request a status

conference in approximately 90 days.
Agnifilo: Given that he'll be in the SHU in the MDC, I can't for now consent to any exclusion under the Speedy Trial Act.

Judge: I can set a trial date if you want. If I can't try it I can find a colleague who can.
Agnifilo: Let me speak with the government...
[He whispers with four AUSAs. Meanwhile Geragos whispering to Sean Combs]
Agnifilo: How about a conference in 14-20 days?

Judge: What's your position on Speedy Trial?
Agnifilo: I'm not prepared to waive it.
Judge: First, the date. Oct 9 at 2 pm.
AUSA: We move to exclude time under the Speedy Trial Act.
Agnifilo: I can't consent. I'll know on October 9.
Judge: I exclude time to then

Judge: We received some calls today from people who say they have evidence for this case. We referred them to the US Attorney's

Office. What about the Local Rule?

AUSA: We wanted to flag defense counsel's comments about the victim - we are not requesting action

Agnifilo: It would be better if he's put in Essex County [Correctional Facility] that in the MDC.

AUSA: The designation authority is entirely given to the BOP. I don't know there is anything the court can do to put its thumb on the scale.

Judge: Get me a joint letter on this by Monday, Sept 23. We are adjourned.

The above is US v. Combs, Part I - Part II and onward coming, by Inner City Press

www.ingramcontent.com/pod-product-compliance
Lightning Source LLC
Chambersburg PA
CBHW070358230526
45471CB00006B/2626